The Space Between

The Point of Connection

Harville Hendrix, PhD
Helen LaKelly Hunt, PhD

Best-Selling Authors of Getting the Love You Want *and* Making Marriage Simple

Clovercroft Publishing

Published by Clovercroft Publishing, Franklin, Tennessee.

Printed in the United States of America

978-1-945507-36-6

Contents

chapter one

It All Began in Technicolor

EVERYONE IS LOOKING FOR some-thing. And, if you've opened this book, this includes you.

That something is a special sensation we had long ago that we dimly remember and can barely describe. It's a longing that seems to come from when we were little, that sometimes reappears in special mo-ments but then disappears. Its transient pres-ence stirs our deepest yearning; its absence stirs our deepest pain. It's always there, in the background of our deepest longings.

1

So we look for it everywhere: achievement, adventure, social status, power, and wealth. But these are spurious substitutes; the feelings fade. None of these evoke the sensation nor satisfy our ancient longing.

A clue to the nature and ubiquity of this sensation was intuited by the poet William Wordsworth, who wrote that we all came into the world "trailing clouds of glory … heaven lies about us in our infancy!" This poetic imagery mirrors our sense of being born into a Technicolor world.

In the first minutes after we were born, most of us were greeted by parents who exclaimed delight, even shedding tears of joy, and began relating to us with great tenderness. They sought to respond to our every move, and when we got upset, they soothed us with gentle songs and cuddling, and everything was all right again. And as they lovingly met our needs, the cells of our bodies began to vibrate with a sensation that did not originate inside of us. It arose,

The World is Alive
with Technicolor.

triggered by the resonating presence of our caretakers. This sensation was the "felt sense" of connecting, created by the quality of our interactions with those who loved us and were committed to our well-being.

Because our caretakers' attuned presence made us feel safe, we became curious about our world and began to explore it with wonder and awe. It was a Technicolor world, that became the playground of our imagination and the domain of our explorations.

Now, we have to ask: What kind of a universe must we be living in for such an experience to be possible? To get an answer, we turn to contemporary science, where we learn that everything in our universe is connecting with everything, everywhere, all the time. The relationship between all things is so intricate that something happening somewhere has an impact everywhere. The term physicists use to describe this fascinating quantum reality is "interconnecting."

But these physicists are not describing connecting as something the universe sometimes does and could stop doing. Connecting is the universe being itself. Connecting is its nature.

This means that the connecting "happening" between the stars, the planets, and all the galaxies is also happening between all human beings and between the synapses of the billions of cells in our brains. What is happening in the universe is happening in us, and what is happening in us is happening in the universe. We are a thread in the fabric of the tapestry of Being. Pull a thread locally and its effect is cosmic.

We are not merely observers of this universe, nor are we residents in it. It is US, and we are IT. And thus we find ourselves being an intricate part of an interactive universe, pulsatingly alive and filled with wonder.

To put it another way: Just as connecting is the universe being the universe, connecting is US being OURSELVES. It is not something we sometimes do and can stop doing. We cannot not be connecting.

Connecting is our nature. It's feeling fully alive, ablaze with color.

So, if we think of connecting as the interaction between any two points in the universe and between any two persons in the world, we can symbolize it as an infinity symbol. As is the universe, so are we!

The Flow of Full Aliveness

When two people connect by being attuned, they experience a pulsating energy flowing back and forth, a "felt sense" that they are a point in an interconnecting universe. That awareness, stimulated by the quality of their interaction, triggers the neural sensation of Full Aliveness.

That is the WHAT we are looking for.

And that's how it was in the beginning. When we were connecting with our caretakers who were attuned to our every need, we relished each moment, savoring "simply being" in a Technicolor world.

All this is possible because CON-NECTING is the foundational Reality that gives birth to all other "realities."

Connecting IS Being.
Being IS Connecting.

The felt sensation of connecting is FULL ALIVENESS. In the pages of this book, we invite you on a journey where once again you'll discover the wonder of being alive.

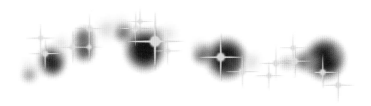

chapter two

But the Lights Went Out

BUT ONE DAY, it all changed. Our Technicolor world faded into shades of gray. Our sensation of full aliveness was replaced with a sort of deadness, dullness, or sometimes a low-grade suffering.

This same theme is found in the origin stories of most great spiritual traditions: It starts out great, and then something goes wrong.

It's the story we all recognize. We've been looking for that sensation in all we aspire to do and be, and so has the rest of human kind.

How did we lose it? What happened that the lights went out?

Here's the story of everyone.

Through no fault of theirs, our doting caretakers eventually became distracted by other things, including their own needs. So there was less playful resonance with them, and as they became unpredictably available, we couldn't count on them being be there for us.

We became disturbed and frightened; and responded by desperately trying to get their attention. But our efforts were futile. And, since our relationship with them was the conduit of our connecting with everything else, when our felt sense of connecting was ruptured, and the Technicolor universe began to fade.

But traces of the original glow were left in our memories, fueling the hope that someday, somewhere, we would experience joyful connecting and Full Aliveness again.

So, the search began and continues until we fall in love, where we find it! Surprisingly though, we lose it again.

You might think we would fall in love with someone with whom we could sustain a loving connection, someone compatible, so that the lights would stay on!

But that is not the way it happens. The mystery is that we fall in love with a person in adulthood who has both the strengths and weaknesses of our caretakers, and the drama of childhood repeats itself all over again.

What a bummer! But hey, we don't like this theory either. The fact is, we've stuggled with this too, so we do know what we are talking about.

So, what specifically in this childhood drama travels with us to adulthood and causes confusion and suffering?

Anxiety. The anxiety that haunts us was triggered by our caretakers, and in adulthood, it escalates when our partner seems preoccupied or upset. The disturbance triggers, in our imagination, the possibility that we might not only lose our connecting with Being, but that we might not "be" at all.

Like joyful aliveness, anxiety also travels our neural pathways, but both feelings cannot co-exist at the same time. In any moment, our brains can experience either joy or terror.

Anxiety, whether mild or severe, is the backdrop of all other human problems. It causes us to turn inward and isolate.

Self-Absorption. We isolate by shutting down our receptors to outside information and become self-absorbed—aware only of what is happening inside us. We are then cut off from the rest of the world and the people we love.

Think of it this way: Imagine you are walking on a beautiful beach at sunset. The majestic waves of the ocean, the glory of the sunset ... But suddenly, you accidentally stub your toe on a very sharp rock, spraining it and perhaps breaking it. OUCH. The majestic waves, the beach, and the sunset suddenly disappear. There is only your poor, aching toe. And until the pain subsides, that is all there is.

So, without information coming in from the outside, we construct other people **as we need them to be**, populating their inner worlds with ours. And when we need them, we expect them to think and feel like us, so that they will do our bidding! And when they resist, we try to force them to meet our expecations.

Polarization between two monads

Objection to Difference. Self-absorption leads to polarization—two people lacking attunement to one another, as illustrated in the two circles above. These two monads fear and object to each other's difference. "Objection to difference" is the fundamental human problem. And, fearing each other, they no longer read each other's inner world and connecting is impossible.

Absence of Empathy. When we cannot feel the emotional state of others, we cannot connect with them, nor they with us. Without receiving data from the other, we lose the capacity to feel their feelings. This dehumanizes them, in our thinking, and we turn them into "objects."

The Rise of Objectification. When we transform a person into an object, we can treat them however we want. We assign expectations to them and inflict punishments if they don't comply.

But everyone, especially our partners, resists being objectified. So we move into a power struggle—a struggle we all recognize—that can last a week or a lifetime.

We all bring these impediments to connecting to our adult lives. All of us are afflicted with these symptoms of anxiety, but because we do not know they come from our own pain, we spend most of our lives trying to get our partner to see things our way and to surrender their view of reality. It's a form of emotional annihilation.

But the reality is that your partner longs to be seen by you just as they are, and to be connected to you. And you feel the same way! If we will regain the capacity to be present for our partner in a loving and attuned way, we will be able to recover joyful connecting and feel the sensation of full aliveness flow once again through our neural wiring.

So this is what flips the switch and turns the lights back on. It returns us to the original gift given us by the universe—found at the Point of Connection.

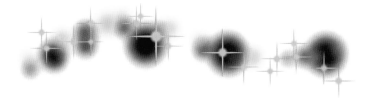

chapter three

Living in the Space Between

NOW THAT WE KNOW *what* we've been looking for, we also want to know *where* it can be found and *how* to get it back.

The *where* is hidden in the middle of your relationship. It's a place you've probably never thought about looking!

Most of us think a relationship is two people interacting. We propose a relationship is "two people and the Space Between them." The Space Between is an energy field that flows between you and your partner. And it's the way two people care for the Space Between that determines the quality of their relationship.

The Space Between? How can that be important? It's empty space. Or is it?

When we look up at the night sky, we're looking into outer space. This Space Between the heavenly bodies was presumed to be empty, until astronomers discovered the powerful energy fields that reside within it. Outer space is filled with dark energy and gravitational pulls that hold up the massive planets, moons, and suns, rotating with exact precision in their orbits. It's the Space Between that choreographs and maintains the heavenly order of the entire universe!

The same holds true for the Space Between two people. Yes, it may be invisible and may appear to be empty, but this relational space is also replete with energy that determines the quality of the space within. The fact is, life is actually lived in the Space Between. It is the energy of the Space Between that populates the world within!

The quality of our relationships determines the quality of our lives.

The Space Between is precisely *where* we recover the sensation of full aliveness and joy.

And the *how*? To understand *how* we get it back, we need to acknowledge the quality of this energy field between us and our Beloved. It all depends on the energy you choose to generate in that space.

We have two choices. We can make the Space Between either safe or dangerous. If the Space Between is safe, connecting will be restored, and we will thrive and feel fully alive. If it is dangerous, we will instinctively feel defensive to protect ourselves. We cannot turn the danger sensors off, even if we want to. We will automatically

List five things you receive
from your partner that
make you feel loved
and cared about.

shrink tightly into a monad state and survive by going it alone.

We may not be aware of ways we evoke danger for our partner. We may rush around, use a harsh tone, roll our eyes, and occasionally shame, blame, or criticize. These negative interactions trigger our partner's anxiety and activate their defenses.

On the other hand, we can choose to make it safe for our partner. We can use a kinder tone of voice, ask our partner how they are feeling, or express gratitude about something that we often take for granted. This respectful quality of interacting affirms our partner as valuable in their own right.

So this is why you have to get it. Safety is non-negotiable. Ultimately, the Space Between is the *where* we recover awareness of connection and full aliveness. It's the quality of our interaction in the Space Between that turns the light back on.

Now the way two people can create safety in the Space Between involves three practices. We will list them here and explore them in greater detail in the next chapters:

★ Use Safe Conversations: A structured process where two people take turns talking and listening. The structure creates safety. Our brains like predictability.

★ Commit to Zero Negativity: A practice that helps you talk without put-downs. It's not what you say; it's how you say it.

★ Offer Affirmations daily: A commitment to bring caring behaviors, surprises, and increased play into your relationship.

These three relational practices not only create a healthier relationship, they also create a healthier brain.

Speaking of the brain, let's close this chapter with some basic brain science.

Generally speaking, the brain can be divided into three sections:

★ The lower, reptilian brain reacts spontaneously, without thinking. Its job is to react to anything dangerous to keep us alive. When it senses danger, it responds with fight, flight, or freeze.

★ The midbrain, or limbic system, processes feelings, emotions, and memories. It's where we experience feeling alive.

★ The upper brain, the neocortex, organizes data, solves problems, and creates win-wins, so that the differences you both have can be honored and respected.

Knowing about these three parts can be helpful. For example, it's fine when the lower brain reacts to danger, but we don't want to stay in that place for long. Fighting, fleeing, or freezing won't get us what we want. It's smart to shift to the upper brain as soon as possible. It is here that we can collaborate together. This is how we can live together in peace.

In recent decades, Neuroscience had two relevant breakthroughs:

First breakthrough—A new term: *neuroplasticity*. This concept suggests our brains are somewhat plastic, in that our neural pathways can actually be reinforced or not, by selecting the thoughts you run through it. Yes, you have the power to change your own brain!

Second breakthrough—A new insight. Our brains are "social." They are shaped and reshaped by our experiences and relationships, especially with those closest to us.

And be aware that different parts of the brain release different neurochemicals. When you feel in danger around your partner, your brain releases cortisol and adrenaline—neurochemicals of fear and anxiety. When you feel safe, your brain releases dopamine, endorphins, and oxytocin—neurochemicals of pleasure that make it feel wonderful to be alive.

The more we create safety, caring, and humor in the Space Between, the more the neurochemicals of well-being, wonder, and Full Aliveness are released.

A good question to ask yourself is, given the way you talk to your partner—your words, tone of voice, and the look in your eye—what neurochemicals get set off in their brains?

Now, to close this chapter, we share a universal law: Energy follows attention. What you focus on is what you get. If you pay attention to the things your partner does wrong, then the neural pathways of anger and fear get reinforced, and the accompanying neurochemicals are released throughout your body. If you focus on your Beloved's positive qualities and the efforts they are making, your brain releases the pleasure neurochemicals. This rewires neural pathways, training your brain to notice *even more* of the good stuff. What is exciting is that this is something you can develop by practicing. How empowering!

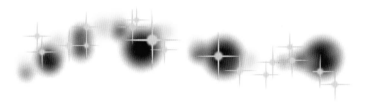

chapter four

Speaking a New Language

EVERY CULTURE HAS ITS own language. The language of the Space Between is Safe Conversations.

Safe Conversations is a new way to talk that creates a relationship of safety, joy, and wonder.

The Space Between is Sacred Space.

Talking is the most dangerous thing people do, and listening is the most infrequent. We need a new way to talk so people will listen and a new way to listen so people will talk.

What makes talking dangerous is the use of Monologue: one person talking and everyone else listening. It's dangerous because it treats those listening as objects who should accept our point of view as truth. Why, then, do a lot of us speak that way? Because our culture rewards us when we talk that way! When we were students, we got better grades when we spoke with conviction and certainty. That led to better jobs and more promotions when we got older. So this Monologue style prevailed, but it results in a top-down dynamic.

Also, no one rewards us if we listen well. So the listener often feels in a one-down position. They then try to restore equal status by rejecting or deflecting the points made. All this does is reverse the one-down position. This mutual devalua-tion triggers anxiety that arouses defenses and leads to conflict and disconnection.

Two monads deflecting each other

And the Technicolor world of full aliveness fades to those dark shades of grey.

The Safe Conversations Process. The good news is that a structure now exists that facil-itates moving from Monologue to Dialogue. Safe Conversations offers the framework where both of you take turns talking. *It is a way of talking without criticism, listening without judging, and connecting through* *differences.* Using this process, you both will feel more respected and heard.

The Safe Conversation process has three parts:

★ Mirroring: Repeating back what your partner said, so their feelings are heard.

★ Validating: Seeing your partner's perspective from their point of view, without surrendering your own.

★ Empathizing: Imagining the feelings your partner had while they were sending their message.

But before using the three parts, however, we engage in the "set up."

The Set Up

★ To begin, choose who will be the Sender (the one who talks) and who will be the Receiver (the one who listens). Don't worry; you'll each have a chance to do both!

★ Sender MAKES AN APPOINTMENT. This may seem excessively formal, but it honors the boundaries of the other person. It helps ensure that the Receiver will be focused on their partner's message. If the Receiver can't give total focus, they can say, "Not now. But I can be available later at X time."

★ Sender and Receiver FACE EACH OTHER. When they do so, their bodies can begin to relate, even before their words do.

★ Next, they MAKE EYE CONTACT, take three deep breaths and allow their eyes to soften into a gaze. Most of the time when you look at each other (especially if you're busy), your eyes might have a glare. Soft pupils say to your partner, "I am open to what you have to say."

When is the last time you and your Beloved took time to gaze into one another's eyes?

The Safe Conversations Process

★ Sender EXPRESSES AN APPRECIATION. Consider your first few Safe Conversations to be a practice! With a few simple words or phrases, send your partner an appreciation (e.g., their appearance, a trait you admire, or a memory of them that you value).

★ Receiver MIRRORS by saying, "If I got it, you said _____." The mirror should be either "word for word" or an "accurate paraphrase," depending upon the preference of the Sender.

★ Receiver CHECKS FOR ACCURACY by saying, "Did I get that?" Some research states that the accuracy listening rate of most of us, even when we are relaxed and focused, hovers around 13 percent.

That means an 87 percent distortion rate, and that is when we are not stressed! Under stress, the distortion rate has to be off the charts! No wonder communication breaks down so easily.

★ Receiver EXPRESSES CURIOSITY. Rather than the typical response, "Are you done yet?" the Receiver asks a magic question: "Is there more about that?" there more about that?" What makes it feel like magic is that it conveys to the Sender, "I have time for you."

★ Receiver SUMMARIZES the Sender's message beginning with the sentence, "Let me see if I got it all."

★ Receiver VALIDATES the Sender's message by saying, "You make sense, and what makes sense is ..."

This doesn't mean the Receiver agrees. It means they recognize that the Sender "makes sense" from their perspective.

★ Receiver EMPATHIZES with Sender by trying to imagine how the Sender is feeling. The Receiver says, "And I can imagine with what you just said, you might be feeling _____." The Receiver might choose from major feelings like sad, mad, glad, or scared. The Receiver then checks it out, saying, "Is that your feeling?" If the Sender says, "No," the Receiver inquires and then mirrors the Sender's feelings, until the Sender feels heard.

★ Receiver then says, "Thanks for sharing all that with me." The Sender says, "Thanks for listening." Connecting is deepened with expressions of gratitude.

SENDER AND RECEIVER NOW SWITCH ROLES—to continue practicing.

After becoming comfortable sharing appreciations using the Safe Conversations structure, you can then use the process with more challenging topics.

Transformation

Safe Conversations helps two people see each other and become more attuned to each other's experience. It helps them develop presence. When two people validate each other, the oscillation between their two worlds amplifies while both maintain their individual essence. This makes Safe Conversations much more than a "communication" tool. It is a process of transformation.

Imagine a world where everyone has the relational skills to keep each other safe!

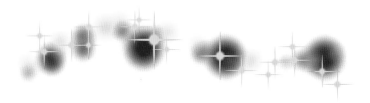

IS THERE MORE?

chapter five

Saying Goodbye to the Bad Stuff

THE RELATIONAL CONCEPT TAUGHT in this chapter sounds almost impossible— Zero Negativity (ZN). What? How can this be? How can I be authentic without dealing with my anger? My partner needs to know how bad they make me feel. How could Zero Negativity be possible?

Well, believe it or not, working toward the state of ZN is the way to go. If you prioritize this non-negotiable practice of the Safe Conversations process, it will bring back the joy you are looking for.

Before we explain the process, let's define what we want *zero* of: *NEGATIVITY.* Negativity is any transaction that one of you experiences as a put-down. If one of you reports it as negative, it *is* negative, whether you intended it as negative or not.

A put-down can be made with body language (turning away or making a gesture), words (shaming, blaming), or tone of voice. **The point is,** *"It's not what you say; it's how you say it."*

Then the big question is, "But if I go Zero Negative, what do I do with all my negative feelings?" The pages ahead will explain how to deal with your frustrations in ways that don't land so negatively on your partner. The more safe you become to your partner, the more they will be open to meeting your needs.

Zero Negativity is looking at everything and everyone through the eyes of Love. When you stay in the ZN consciousness long enough, the other appears in their pristine reality: They appear as wondrous. Wonder and negativity are incompatible. It's Wonder and Zero Negativity that correlate.

You can't feel negativity and Full Aliveness at the same time!

But the fact is that it's hard to make it through even one day with no negativity. We all blow it! That's because our brains have been conditioned for millennia to be slightly paranoid. This served to help our ancient ancestors discern whether others were coming for a friendly dinner or to have them for dinner! This millennia of programming results in us being wary of the intention of others. When our partner does something that feels negative to us, it instinctively triggers the amygdala—the fear center of our brains—and floods our brain with cortisol and adrenalin. Our instinctual first response is to defend ourselves and fight back.

THINK OF SOMETHING THAT
was said to you
THAT MADE  WHAT
You FEEL was
PUT
DOWN SAID?
HOW DID IT MAKE YOU FEEL?

WHAT DO YOU WISH THEY HAD SAID INSTEAD?

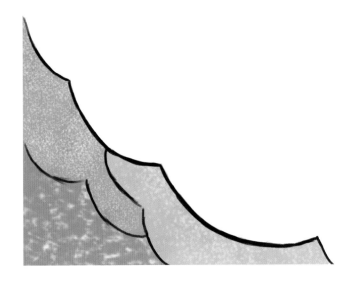

While it's difficult to control our first thought, we *can* control our second thought. We can implement a Repair Process that helps restore connection. Repair should be made as soon as possible.

If, in your relationship, one of you experiences negativity, that person should signal that they have experienced a put-down. The word used as a signaling device needs to be agreed upon by the two of you. The "ZN signal" might be an "ouch," "oops," "wow," "bing," or whatever you think might work. The two of us use "bing" (said gently).

When one of you expresses a "bing," stop, make an appointment, and use the ZN Repair process. The person who experienced the bing then becomes the Sender. The other person, now the Receiver, must take the ZN feedback of the Sender.

The Sender, using a kind voice, tells the Receiver what feels negative. The Receiver simply receives the feedback, practices "curiosity," and offers to do a repair.

THE ZERO NEGATIVITY REPAIR PROCESS

The Repair Process includes four options.

★ The Redo or Do-Over. The Sender resends the message in a way that's not experienced as so negative.

★ Modeling. The Receiver models the redo, using the behavior, words, tone of voice, facial expression, and so on that they wish their partner would have used.

★ Relational Behaviors. In many cases, an apology or a hug may be sufficient. But flowers or chocolate might also help!

★ The Full Dialogue. You might want a dialogue, so that the reason for the put-down can be explored, and the reason for sensitivity to the put-down can be communicated.

ALSO, TAKE CARE OF YOU and your relationship! If intense negative interactions are frequent, seek out a professional counselor/therapist/coach.

We often use the metaphor of a clean, flowing river to communicate the care needed in a relationship. The Space Between is your beautiful flowing river. The last thing you want to do is dump oily toxins, nasty acid, or dangerous chemicals into the water. Toxins destroy the safety in the Space Between. Water should be refreshing and life-giving! Practicing ZN allows you to keep the pristine water flowing freely, allowing the Space Between to be a place of beauty and peace.

And by the way, we both know what it's like to be miserable in a relationship. Sadly, we were actually talking to divorce attorneys. Finally, we created this ZN process and practiced it daily. And, we turned our relationship around. It was amazing!

Now remember: You won't ever have a relationship that is completely Zero Negative. Those accidental put-downs are just

THE SPACE
BETWEEN
is like a
river

Don't dump
TOXINS
in there
OR ELSE...

COMMIT TO
ZERO NEGATIVITY
and LOOK
what happens

going to happen. The most important point is that *the sign of a healthy relationship is quick repair.*

And while learning ZN takes daily practice, when this skill is acquired, you can both shift from conflict to connection much more quickly. And you both will begin to feel such triumph! In our case, it used to take a week (or sometimes three!) to repair an ouch or bing. Now, with the Repair Process, we can do it right away. It does take commitment and focus, but you can learn to do it too! It truly can be a joyful skill to acquire.

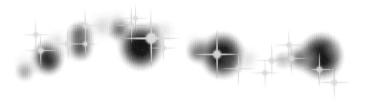

chapter six

Saying Hello to the Good Stuff

BUT LISTEN; IT'S NOT enough to go Zero Negative (ZN). You have to go positive too, big time! It's like a field of weeds. You have to replace weeds with different seeds to get what you want. And a sure way to create positivity in your relationship is to commit to daily affirmations. So no matter how you are feeling about your partner, make several comments **each day** about the things they are doing right.

Now this may seem like a tall order, but it is in your own best interest. Here's why. Early on, we asked "What kind of universe would it have to be for the experience of full aliveness to be possible?" We noted that quantum physics claims that "interconnecting" is the fundamental feature of our universe, and that the action of anything anywhere impacts everything everywhere. How this translates to our relationships is that whatever we do to another person is done to us.

> Affirmation and Negation cannot travel the same neural pathways at the same time.

So here are the two great learnings from the physics of our universe. 1) You can't hurt another person without hurting yourself. It also follows that 2) when you give an Affirmation, you experience that same Affirmation. Our universe is designed in such a way that we cannot cheat. Whatever we focus on is what returns to us.

So, if we want to live in a Technicolor world, we **can** turn the lights back on. By now you know where the light switch is! It's in the Space Between that is becoming Zero Negative. Daily Affirmations will help to bring back the joy. It's empowering to know we have the choice to turn on the lights whenever we want.

One more thing! Did you know that couplehood can be a spiritual path? For those to whom their faith or spiritual tradition is important, your marriage can be a place you practice the presence of God daily. You may be feeling sad or anxious about something. But stop for a minute. Your partner may be feeling the same way! So instead of focusing just on yourself, spend time each day offering a few acts of kindness to your partner, whether they deserve it or not! Ask yourself, what can I do to affirm my partner today?

Write five things that you appreciate about your partner that you haven't mentioned recently.

An Affirmation is something you do that will help your partner feel more safe in your relationship. Examples are offering a hug, saying words of appreciation, engaging in spontaneous play, giving surprises, and offering support for the dreams of the other.

God has given you one person in the whole wide world to love, help heal, and help grow. Your partner is longing for you to be that one person who will be their advocate when all else fails. And as you create a plan for sharing daily Affirmations, you can structure "On Duty Days," where you each take turns being "responsible" to make sure affirmations are exchanged, This helps the day end with the two of you connected.

So, practice cultivating beauty and joy with each other. Keep the flow between you fresh and beautiful. When you do, the "river between you" can also reflect the light of the sun during the day and the peaceful, beautiful moon at night.

Four Ways to Bring More Affirmations into Your Life

Again co-create a plan so that loving moments can be experienced with more predictability in your relationship. Then tape the plan on a mirror you both look at often.

★ Offer Appreciations on a Daily Basis. Appreciations can be about anything your partner did that day—paying the bills, taking out the trash, tidying up the kitchen sink, or showing up on time.

★ Remember that the more you share these appreciations, the more you are likely to receive. So practice saying a few times a day: "One thing I appreciate about you is ..."

★ Offer Caring Behaviors that make you each feel cared about and loved. Examples include foot massage, special home-cooked dinner, words of appreciation, special gifts, and date nights. Tell your partner what makes you feel loved and cared about. It empowers them to know exactly how they can have a positive impact on you.

★ Exchanging Surprises can be planned! Surprises trigger bonding neurochemicals, which bring increased joy and safety in the Space Between. You might want to conduct a "surprise inventory" and simply ask, "What would surprise you if I did it?" and then write down what you learn.

Also, you can make a list of "random droppings." Simply pay attention to off-handed comments your partner makes—things they would like to do or own, or something they would like you to do for them, sometime—somewhere!

Anticipation is an often-forgotten source of delight.

★ Create High-Energy Fun together.

List some surprises
that you would
cherish and enjoy.

We define fun as any activity that produces a belly laugh or an orgasm or maybe even both at the same time. Ha!

Fun activity includes reading joke books, watching silly comedies on TV, wearing Groucho Marx glasses, playful teasing, making faces, and dancing. If you are "fun-impaired," as we were years ago, program fun into your life. We did, and we discovered that laughter is the hallmark of a thriving relationship.

And don't forget: Safety is essential for a thriving relationship. If it's safe, the neuro-chemicals of love flow through our bodies, and we want to be with that person again! But if it's scary or dangerous, cortisol is released, our defenses automatically rise, and we move away, which causes the rupture.

You don't need to be a rocket scientist to see the wisdom of daily Affirmations!

As each of you think about
your dream relationship,
list five things that you
both agree that you
would like to be
doing together.

Predictable Affirmations sustain safety and connecting. We have the power to foster safety and joy each moment of our day by the decisions we make at the Point of Connection.

What if we told you that you can actually have the relationship of your dreams? Well, it's not going to happen unless you make a plan for it, which will help the dream become manifest. The Proverbs state, "Where there is no vision, the people perish"—the same is true for your relationship. Dreaming together and casting a vision for your future includes making concrete plans and goals.

Here's how it's done. Each of you take some paper and imagine what life could be like for you as a couple in the future. List specific things you see the two of you doing in your dream relationship—ways you take care of your physical bodies, ways you have fun together, trips you want to take. After you both complete your individual lists, compare and see what you both agree on. Then put those activities on another sheet—and you have the beginning of your dream relationship. You can fill it out with more detail over time.

In the meantime, practice affirming the good memories and all you currently appreciate as you both take steps toward co-creating your dream relationship.

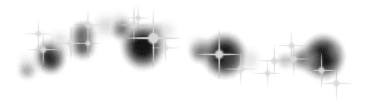

chapter seven

Managing Your Fears

ALL OF US HAD imperfect parenting. Our parents had imperfect parenting too. Being raised by imperfect parents, we experienced a "Childhood Challenge."

Patterns that we developed as children with our caretakers tend to show up in our present-day relationships. Once you learn more about your partner's past challenges, you will likely see them in a more empathic way. Your partner might grow to understand you better, too.

Which kind of Childhood Challenge did you have? Intrusive or Neglectful? Circle one.

MY EARLY CHALLENGE

When the major caretaker was...

INTRUSIVE
I Wanted:

- To get free from feeling controlled by others.

- To express my own thoughts rather than being told what I should think.

- To express what I felt, rather than what I should feel.

- To experience my thoughts and feelings as important.

- To do what I wanted to do rather than what I ought to do.

NEGLECTFUL
I Wanted:

- To experience feeling seen and valued.

- To be approached by others rather than being left alone/abandoned.

- To feel significant as a person.

- To get support for what I think or feel.

- To feel someone is interested in what I want and like.

Generally speaking, each of us came from caretakers who were either too Intrusive or too Neglectful. They were either "in our face" all the time, telling us what to do, think, and feel. Or they weren't there very much, physically, emotionally, or both. This became your "Childhood Challenge."

Share with each other what you circled about your Childhood Challenge using the Safe Conversations process. This can be a very tender and informative experience for you both. You will learn more about why your partner does the things they do and feels the way they feel.

MY CHILDHOOD DEFENSE

Given that these challenges were painful, we all created a defense against the pain.

Defending ourselves, we typically reacted in one of two ways. We either:

⭐ **Minimized our feelings.** We pulled them in, so we could process them. Or:

⭐ **Maximized our feelings.** We needed to talk a lot about them and process our feelings with others.

In the Safe Conversations paradigm, we call the person who minimizes their feelings a Minimizer, and the person who maximizes, a Maximizer.

And in Safe Conversations, we have two adorable names for these two character types:

The Minimizer is called a Turtle.

The Maximizer is called a Hail Storm.

Inevitably, these two character types are drawn like magnets to be with each other.

Incompatibility is the grounds for marriage.

Yes, The Turtle is drawn to the Hail Storm's high energy, and the Hail Storm is drawn to the Turtle's solid grounding. You can see how that would be exciting and cozy in the beginning. But over time, the qualities that attracted can begin to irritate! And problems that surface in your relationship can become more complicated if you don't become aware of these different styles of defenses.

We suggest you use these designations because they can be helpful. When a problematic issue arises, one of you will tend to pull inward like a Turtle, and the other will tend to become expressive, like a Hail Storm.

Once conscious of this dynamic, you can influence one another—that is, determine how much the Hail Storm hails and note how far the Turtle retreats into their shell. When you both become attuned to each other, it really helps calm everything down!

Here is what to do:

First, decide which one you are. (Remember, it becomes particularly clear when a problem surfaces.) And then create plans, so your partner doesn't escalate into their defensive posture.

Which are you?

A message to the Hail Storm—If you, the Hail Storm, notice the Turtle retreating into their shell, don't hail on them. That will cause your poor Turtle to retreat all the more. Plan something to do that you enjoy—find a new hobby, start reading a great book, or call a friend. Pick some activity you can truly enjoy to take your mind off the situation. If you use patience, your Turtle will soon come out of their shell, more available to address the problems. They will also be deeply appreciative that you have waited until they were available to work on solutions together.

A message to the Turtle—Take heart, you Turtles! Your Beloved is worried and upset. The more you withdraw and shut out your partner, the more they will increase the hailing and the storm! This is a great time to ask them if there is something you might do for them. Try mirroring them and then validate their point of view. This helps the storm clouds dissipate and the bright glowing sun return! You will be much happier once you've helped your Hail Storm calm the storm.

We have three suggestions as we close this chapter:

Using Safe Conversations should help you as a Turtle talk more in the relationship, sharing your gifts, rather than going into your shell. Using Safe Conversations should help you as the Hail Storm stop hailing, so the love and warmth you so want to give, will be gratefully received.

Be sure to use "Sender Responsibility" when you send your message. This means use succinct sentences and use a pleasant tone of voice. Both Hail Storms and Turtles can tend to flood their partner with words, and then your partner shuts down. The point is to learn to speak succintly, so that your Beloved can succeed at mirroring you.

Finally, do seek out a counselor or a therapist if you need one. They might help

you create a plan so you can live more easily with this dynamic.

Life is lived in the Space Between.

And it's good to remember that Nature
itself is dyadic. It is replete with co-existing
polarities—the yin and yang, hot and cold,
dark and light, up and down. We are wired
to seek out our opposite. So don't blame
your partner for the way they are. After all,
you picked them! Try shifting your attitude
about their differences. Once they feel
more accepted by you, they will begin to
adore you for it!

This way, both the Turtle and Hail
Storm can live happily ever after.

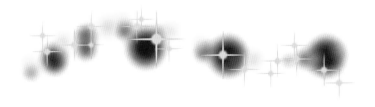

chapter eight

Converting Frustrations Into Wishes

WE'VE BEEN TALKING A lot about connection. But what about conflict? It helps if you remember that conflict is growth trying to happen.

All couples have conflict—either minor, serious, or very serious. Your partner does things that frustrate you, which is something that we need to address.

Frustrations result from one partner doing things that irritate, insult, disappoint, or bother the other.

The other partner reacts by using negativity: shame, blame, or criticism:

"You were late!"

"You always want it your way."

"You didn't shut the back door!"

"I can't believe you just said that."

"When are we going to have sex?"

"You always . . ." "You never . . ."

So the first thing to do to break this destructive cycle is realize that dumping frustrations is toxic to your partner.

A frustration is a Wish in disguise.

It's a smart couple that learns to convert their frustrations into requests for what they want. If the frustration is reframed as a Wish, it invites the co-creation of a solution between the two of you, in the Space Between! And if this Wish is granted, you will feel more safe and respected in your relationship.

The process of converting a frustration into a Wish should include making an appointment to 1) briefly name the frustration and 2) state the Wish and the requests you have. Here's how it goes:

- ★ Set up a Safe Conversations appointment to deal with your frustration.

- ★ When the time has been granted, state the frustration briefly with no negativity and using "I" language. Then state your Wish.

- ★ Make specific SMART Requests of behaviors your partner could do to bring about your Wish. Your partner will choose one. This leads to a co-creation of a solution you both agree to.

The best way to make a request is to be SMART about it. Here's what makes up a SMART Request:

Specific—a behavior

Measurable—observable, quantifiable

Attainable—a small step

Relevant—applicable to the frustration or desire

Time-limited—such as daily for the next two weeks

Then share these requests in a Safe Conversation.

Changing a frustration into a Wish will work wonders in keeping the Space Between safe. This practice removes the toxins that eradicate safety.

More often than not, as we have said, once the romance fades, a power struggle begins, and a couple begins to treat each other like objects. Only when they become intentional and commit to care about the

Both of you list five of your favorite memories with your partner.

needs of each other will they stretch to meet each other's needs. To truly honor your Beloved's Wish, you'll have to stretch beyond your comfort level. But only then do two people truly begin the journey to real love.

> When two people commit to treat each other as an "I–Thou," the universal energy of Love begins to flow through the two people and then into the Space Between.

The Jewish mystic and philosopher Martin Buber was mesmerized by the meaning and significance of relationships. His book *I and Thou* is now a classic. His thesis was that most people treat their partner like an "It," an object to meet their own needs. But when two people shift and begin to respond to the needs of each other in a sacrificial way, their partner becomes a

"Thou," and then the universal energy of love starts to flow through the two people and into the Space Between.

We need to grow into offering each other *agape* love, an unconditional love that transcends our challenges. This sacrificial love emerges in your relationship when there is a shift, and you begin to see your partner as a "Thou," someone to be respected and honored. When this transformation happens, a Love from on High can then become manifest in both of your lives.

The shift from "I" to "Thou" moves you from the lower brain to the upper brain. When frustrated about our own needs, we want to lash out at our partner: Blame, shame, and criticize. This is lower-brain living, which ruptures connection. By reframing a frustration as a Wish and making a SMART Request, you can help your partner focus on small, doable steps they can take in response.

Making requests puts you into your upper brain, where you can continue to creatively co-create solutions as the days go by. A request made SMARTly and communicated with Sender Responsibility—that is, succinctly and with a kind tone of voice— treats your Beloved with the dignity and respect they deserve!

One last point: Safe Conversations is a relational education process, not therapy. If you have serious struggles in your relationship, do seek out a counselor or therapist, who can help you succeed when you use this process.

All this can help you experience a transformation in the Space Between , as it grows to become Sacred Space. And don't forget: Conflict is growth trying to happen.

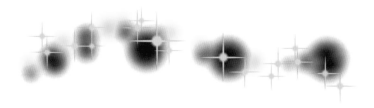

chapter nine

Shifting from Judgment to Wonder

JUDGMENT IS NECESSARY IN sports competitions and determines verdicts in a court of law. Unfortunately, when judgment is used by either of you in your relationship, sadly both of you lose.

Judgment erodes safety. Unless your partner specifically asks for your advice or a critique, it can make them feel disliked, disrespected, or insecure. The joyful flow in the Space Between stops and becomes blocked. Judgment triggers your partner's armored defenses. The reptilian lower brain goes on red alert, reacts, and wants to fight back. Keep judging, and you won't be in relationship with your partner. You'll be in relationship with your partner's defenses.

Judgment suggests that you are the expert about who your partner should be and what they should be doing. This is especially true when we judge how our partner should be acting and relating, so that *your* life works better. But as we have said, our resistance to accepting difference truly is *the problem* in all relational issues. When couples express at the altar "you and I are one," each is secretly hoping, "I'm the one."

Accepting difference is our greatest challenge.

We expect our partner to think, behave, and react like we do. When they don't, we are shocked by their totally unacceptable behavior!

So how do we stop judging? Believe it or not, it requires us to "not-know" our partner. Now that sounds strange. What does it mean to "not-know"?

Clearly, we do know a lot about our partner. Some of their favorite foods and music, some ways they relax. Our partner wants us to know these things. Yet the best way to improve your relationship is to be more curious about them and to ask questions.

When the landscape around us becomes too familiar, we can lose our capacity to be impressed, astonished, and awed. Becoming curious about the "otherness" of our partner allows us to discover new things all the time. Do we know fully why our partner thinks the way they think? We sense what our partner feels, but do we really know the deeper reasons why they feel that way? Try asking them.

You now know that it's good to mirror your partner when they share a thought, see if you got it, and ask them, "Is there more?" This evokes in us a state of curiosity about our partner, which they appreciate.

There is even a special kind of curiosity that is called *Wonder.* The word *Wonder* has two meanings: 1) The verb, as in, "I wonder what we'll do this weekend"; and 2) the noun, as in, "I suddenly realize my partner is a *Wonder.*"

There was a time when you might have seen your Beloved in this wondrous way. You two could talk all night and *still* feel like there were a million things left unexplored. Unlike the tarnish on a relationship gone dull, the romantic phase feels glowing and exciting. What most couples don't know is that even though the romance has faded, you can actually recover these feelings of romance and Wonder.

Every person has a galaxy within them—a reflection of the vast and unknowable space that swirls around our personal solar system. Your partner longs to be both wondered about and seen as a Wonder. This cannot happen until you intentionally practice a "not-knowing" of them.

The best way to "know" your partner is by "not-knowing" them!

Neuroscientists made a discovery: "tolerating ambiguity is a sign of brain health." This not-knowing of our partner helps us integrate and strengthen our own brain. Using the phrase "Is there more?" with your partner helps you ascend to the neocortex, the rational part of your brain, by repeating word for word. This then calms the amygdala and the reactivity of the lower brain. And then, "tolerating ambiguity" will lead to Wonder, awe, and the sense of well-being.

Tolerating ambiguity is a sign of brain health.

Amazingly, this is something you can practice. The power of listening deeply to your partner, devoid of labeling or judging, can become a wondrous experience.

A practice for experiencing Wonder in your relationship is a three-minute process you can do every day. We call it the Ladder to Wonder. Commit a few minutes to this together before bedtime. Put the smartphones down. If you have children, they've gone to bed, so you two have uninterrupted time. Forget about the millions of things that need to be done around the house.

And now exchange the words on the Ladder to Wonder with each other each night. This may feel awkward at first, but before you realize it, a sense of awe will be

Commit: Each night for a month, say these sentences to each other. Start at the bottom. Go one by one to the top. Over time, note how your feelings change.

catalyzed within your relationship. Then, things will never be the same!

Developing Wonder takes practice

Wonder moves us past the desire to understand what things and concepts are. When you define something, you limit it, in a way imprison it, by its definition. With definitions, you are limited by words, by a state of knowing, but Wonder goes beyond words to the state of not knowing. There is something so wondrous in not having the words to express what we are trying to say.

This practice of cultivating the inexplicable phenomena of Wonder moves us from seeing our partner as an object to recognizing them as a most unique and special being in the universe—as one you have the honor to care for and love. Wondering about your partner helps create a wondrous relationship. It is the micro human experience that resonates with the macro of the pulsating and interconnecting cosmos.

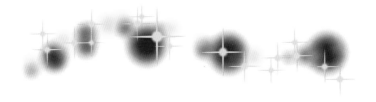

The Universal Energy of
Love Can Flow Through
You Both and Come to
Live in The Space Between.

chapter ten

Living a New Set of Values

IT MAY HAVE DAWNED on you by now that we are talking about something *big*—not just a new idea for your relationship or some new skills to try, but a whole new way to live.

It's time we recognize that the most important thing in our lives is how we care for our relationships. Because it's the quality of our relationships that determines the quality of our lives.

Now that you have learned how to have Safe Conversations with your Beloved, you can see how easy it is to apply Safe Conversations to all relationships. And there is a good reason to do so. Healthy relationships are proven to improve lives by bolstering mental, physical, and financial health. The benefits include:

★ overall happiness, health, and success
★ children's confidence and productivity at school
★ financial well-being

To have healthy relationships, look again at nature. There is no sameness in the universe. Every snowflake is different; not one is a copy. Rather than resisting difference, there are great reasons to explore being curious. Difference is the defining feature of nature. As we seek to embrace it, we open our lives to new possibilities.

In the old way of living, difference evoked feelings of distrust, competition, and control. In the new way of living, difference invites collaboration, cooperation, and co-creation. Difference becomes the basis of growth when people learn to talk without defensiveness. Safe Conversations makes it possible to talk with anyone about anything without polarizing.

Understanding the importance of safety in the Space Between, we realize the value of Zero Negativity (ZN) and Affirmations in all conversations even more. These practices are relevant with family members, with co-workers, in political settings, and with anyone. We can imagine Safe Conversations not just in houses in our neighborhoods, but in the House of Congress. Imagine it as protocol in the presidential debates!

We posit that a commitment to Safe Conversations could transform any ecosystem. Many children who have learned these skills not only enjoy using them with their peers, but help their parents stay on track!

Research suggests that a work environment where everybody feels connected to the team experiences greater productivity. Healthy relationships contribute to workplace satisfaction, a decrease in absenteeism, a reduction in medical complaints, and less conflict, plus overall improvement of the bottom line. More money!

These relational gains are possible because Safe Conversations is something you do rather than a topic to discuss. Think of it as the flavor of the water, not the water or the glass. It is the atmosphere in the room, not the floor, the ceiling, or the wall. It is the grease that removes the squeak from the wheel. It is a quality that transforms whatever it touches.

It's exciting to realize that the integration of Safe Conversations into all our interactions can help create a whole new world, one in which everyone has the chance to thrive. We both truly believe this will come about, if not in our lifetimes, in the next generation.

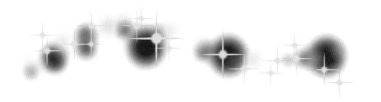

chapter eleven

Creating a Relational Civilization

IMAGINE!

If Safe Conversations could spread everywhere, everyone would feel more safe and regain their sense of full aliveness.

With safety everywhere, we could connect beyond our differences and recognize the innate value of everyone.

The innate value of everyone could then be the basis for a new ethical system that guarantees equality of opportunity for all. An ethic of mutual concern would be expressed as mutual care. Everyone would recognize that we're all born in relationship, injured in relationship, and are healed only in relationship.

Currently, we live in a very different reality.

In our current social and political realty, most of us tend to focus on ourselves and compete with others for available resources. Others are our opponents with whom we compete, or they become resources for meeting our needs. Our interactions with others are tactical and strategic rather than relational. And inequality divides us by social class, race, gender, and economics. The world for most of us consists of shades of gray with occasional glimmers of Technicolor.

This raises a very big question: If Connecting is Being assigns inherent equality to all human beings, how did we wind up like this?

The answer is culture! A culture is essentially a value system that determines how we live together as individuals and in community, and it explains the human condition.

The value system of our culture emerged about 250 years ago, after the wars for democracy that raged in France and America. For ten thousand years prior to the 18th century, everyone was owned by someone else—emperor, king, lord, husband. Authority, as the center of this value system, required obedience and service from everyone else.

In the democracies that arose out of the fallen empires, the identity of persons shifted from that of "subject" who owned nothing, including themselves, to a "self" who was independent and self-sufficient with freedom to pursue their own destiny.

This value gave birth to all the institutions of Western civilization, based on the welfare of the "individual." And this requires constant interpersonal competition and creates social and economic inequality.

We call this the Paradigm of the Individual. It worked, at first. For 250 years, we have admired and supported a cultural system in which everyone was free and encouraged to be their best.

However, this paradigm is not working so well anymore. The "individual" has given way to "individualism," and our culture has devolved into a system of competition, control, and domination, and a "winner-take-all" mindset that clearly places our value on *me* rather than *we*.

All this has created a world of power, privilege, and resources undreamed of by most patriarchs in the past. But it has created so much fragmentation that nearly all the institutions that originally served us are in decay. The decay is so severe that we are now witnessing severe damage to our natural world, rampant social and economic inequality, dysfunctioning educational institutions, and the breakdown of the family. This construct appears now to be ineffective for the future of our civilization and our planet.

However, out of the debris of the Individual Paradigm, we are witnessing the emergence of the Relational Paradigm. It is a concrete expression of Connecting as Being. This emerging shift has implications for the joy of everyone, where the well-being of all is the ethic of the culture. Only with a relational value system can the welfare of the individual and our planet be assured.

By making relationships first, energy and information oscillate between self and other in the Space Between. This oscillation is where strength and power lie. The well-being of the whole ultimately serves the interests of the self, not the other way around!

When we put Relationships First and practice Safe Conversations in the Space Between, we co-create a relational value system that insures the welfare and equality of everyone.

Look at everyone through the eyes of Love.

When this new way of life reaches the tipping point, all social systems will mirror the structure of nature where everything is connecting. The "felt experience" that we belong to a connecting universe will return us all to the wonder and joyful aliveness with which we all began.

Thoughts to Take with You

WE STARTED THIS BOOK with the statement that because we are a part of an interconnecting universe, interacting is our essence. It is our nature to be in relationship. We labeled this foundational reality Connecting is Being. And when we experience the reality of our interconnected state, the sensation of Full Aliveness travels our neural pathways, and we experience joy and wonder.

Second, we stated that our original experience of this sensation occurred when we were babies connecting to our caretakers. And that access to this experience today is dependent upon the quality of our relationship with those we most love.

Third, we noted that while it is our nature to feel fully alive, most of us don't because the inevitable rupture in childhood triggered anxiety and changed our world to black and white. The loss of Full Aliveness became the driver behind everything we do in life.

Fourth, we celebrate the fact that we can restore Full Aliveness when we learn how to see and be seen by those we most love. When we are connecting with others, we re-experience Full Aliveness and our world once again radiates in Technicolor.

There's a new science that helps people transform conflict into connection. The science has become so accessible in recent years that it should be required for a couple who gets a marriage license. Shouldn't couples, like drivers, have to read a manual and pass a test before they take in the responsibility and challenge of living with another person?

Also, the science is now so simple, even kids can use it. Some of our colleagues say there should be four *R*'s in school: reading, writing, arithmetic, and relationship.

So now, let's look to the future. You are equipped to use and share the new relational science that helps people from conflict to connecting through differences. Let's imagine. Think of all the unnecessary suffering we could prevent or ameliorate if this new relational science became a new way of life around the world.

Harville + Helen

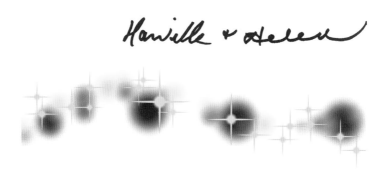

About the Authors

HARVILLE HENDRIX, PhD, and HELEN LAKELLY HUNT, PhD, are life partners who want to make relational information and skills available to everyone. They co-created Imago Relationship Therapy and co-initiated Imago Relationships International as a training institute for couples' therapists. They co-founded Relationships First as a collaborative mission to create a relational culture and Safe Conversations® as a social experiment to raise the joy index in a city.

They believe that how we interact with each other is the key to the emotional, physical, economic, and relational well-being of everyone. They envision shifting from the age of the individual to the age of relationships.

Over 1,200 Imago therapists practice in thirty-seven countries. Their professional partnership has produced ten books, including three *New York Times* best sellers: *Getting the Love You Want*, *Keeping the Love You Find*, and *Giving the Love That Heals*. Their latest book is *Making Marriage Simple* (2013).

Dr. Hendrix is a couple's therapist with over forty years' experience as an educator, clinical trainer, and lecturer. Dr. Hunt is author of *Faith and Feminism* and has been inducted into the National Women's Hall of Fame in Seneca Falls, New York, for her leadership in the women's movement.

Helen and Harville have been married for over thirty years and have six amazing children and reside in Dallas, Texas.

Safe Conversations
A Course for Couples

Discover the six-week couples course that people are calling "life-changing," "transformative," and "powerful."

Join Harville and Helen for a life-changing experience to rekindle the wonder, magic, and joy in your relationships. Using their revolutionary Relationship Methodology, proven to strengthen the bond between couples, they weave together expert teaching, inspirational stories, practical tips, engaging demonstrations, and powerful activities to help you and your partner experience the joy you deserve.

In this six-session course, you and your partner will learn how to:

Feel safe, valued, and connected in your relationship.

Increase the joy in your relationships at home, work, and everywhere.

Use simple yet powerful communication techniques for having an effective – and safe – conversation.

Co-create your dream relationship.

Express frustrations in a new way that turns conflict into connection.

Rediscover the fun, romance, and wonder of life with

Safe Conversations: A Course for Couples.

Go to www.relationshipsfirst.org

If you'd like to find out more about Imago Relationhip Therapy or to find an Imago Therapist in your area go to *http://imagorelationships.org/*